CUSTOMER SERVICE EXCELLENCE

Edge Hill University

Learning Services

Edge Hill University

LEARNING SERVICES

Renew Online: http://library.edgehill.ac.uk

24/7 telephone renewals: 01695 58 4333

Help line: 01695 58 4286

Looking at Countries
POLAND

Kathleen Pohl

FRANKLIN WATTS
LONDON • SYDNEY

First published in 2009
by Franklin Watts

Franklin Watts
338 Euston Road
London NW1 3BH

Franklin Watts Australia
Level 17/207 Kent Street
Sydney, NSW 2000

First published in 2009 by Gareth Stevens Publishing
1 Reader's Digest Road
Pleasantville
NY 10570-7000 USA

Dewey number: 914.38
ISBN: 978 0 7496 8248 4

Senior Managing Editor: Lisa M. Herrington
Senior Editor: Barbara Bakowski
Creative Director: Lisa Donovan
Designer: Tammy West
Photo Researcher: Charlene Pinckney

Photo credits: (t=top, b=bottom, l=left, r=right, c=centre)
Cover (main) © Keren Su/Corbis; cover (inset) © Jenny Matthews/Alamy; title page Shutterstock; p. 4
© lookGaleria/Alamy; p. 6 © Momatiuk-Eastcott/Corbis; p. 7t Hellier Robert Harding World
Imagery/Getty Images; p. 7b © blickwinkel/Alamy; p. 8t © Paul Springett/Alamy; p. 8b © Caro/Alamy;
p. 9 © age fotostock/SuperStock; p. 10 © Jenny Matthews/Alamy; p. 11t © Steve Skjold/Alamy; p. 11b
Czarek Sokolowski/AP; p. 12 Piotr Malecki/Getty Images; p. 13t © mediacolor's/Alamy; p. 13b Piotr
Malecki/Getty Images; p. 14t © age fotostock/SuperStock; p. 14b © Lech Muszyñski/PAP/Corbis; p. 15
© lookGaleria/Alamy; p. 16 © Dallas and John Heaton/Free Agents Limited/Corbis; p. 17t © Atlantide
Phototravel/Corbis; p. 17b © Steve Skjold/Alamy; p. 18 © lookGaleria/Alamy; p. 19 Gehman/National
Geographic/Getty Images; p. 20t © Ryman Cabannes/photocuisine/Corbis; p. 20b © Barry
Lewis/Alamy; p. 21 Krzysztof Dydynski/Lonely Planet Images; p. 22 © JTB Photo Communications,
Inc./Alamy; p. 23t © Peter Andrews/Reuters/Corbis; p. 23b © Barbara Ostrowska/PAP/Corbis; p. 24t ©
Grzegorz Momot/PAP; p. 24b Kacper Pampel/Reuters/Landov; Corbis; p. 25 © Darek
Delmanowicz/EPA/Corbis; pp. 26–27 Shutterstock (3). Every attempt has been made to clear
copyright. Should there be any inadvertent omission please apply to the publisher for rectification.

Printed in China

Franklin Watts is a division of Hachette Children's Books,
an Hachette Livre UK company.
www.hachettelivre.co.uk

Contents

Where is Poland?

Poland is in central Europe. It shares borders with seven countries. To the west is Germany and to the south are the Czech Republic and Slovakia. Poland's neighbours to the east are Ukraine, Belarus and Lithuania. In the north, Poland borders Russia. Poland's coastline is on the Baltic Sea.

Did you know?

Poland's present borders were set after the Second World War (1939–45).

The land boundaries of Poland have changed over the years, often due to war or invasion. At times, Poland has even disappeared off the map.

The Sejm in Warsaw is the Polish parliament, where politicians meet.

Baltic Sea

POLAND

EUROPE

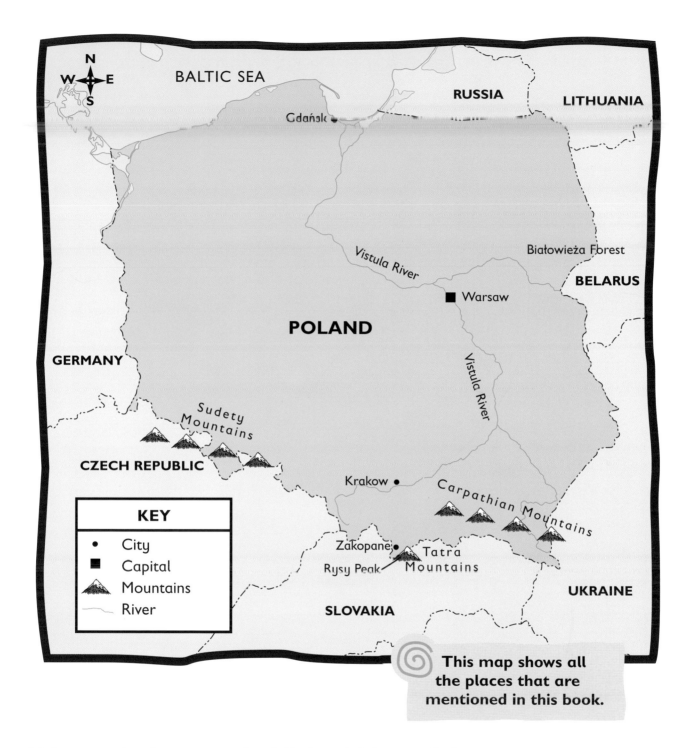

This map shows all the places that are mentioned in this book.

Warsaw is the capital of Poland. Most of the city was badly damaged during the Second World War. Some parts of Warsaw were rebuilt to look as they did in the past. Other parts are a mixture of old castles and modern buildings.

The landscape

Long stretches of flat land called plains make up most of Poland. There are also forests and bogs – areas of wet, spongy ground. There are thousands of small lakes in the north. Sandy beaches line Poland's coast on the Baltic Sea.

Did you know?

An area of northern Poland is called the 'Land of a Thousand Lakes'. The lakes formed thousands of years ago, during the last Ice Age. Most of northern Europe was covered with ice then.

The plains make good farm land for growing crops.

Bison are the biggest land animals in Europe. They live in the Białowieża Forest in north-east Poland and Belarus.

Most Polish people, or Poles, live in the central plains. Rolling farm land covers most of that area. Some of the biggest cities are there, too, including Warsaw. The Vistula River, Poland's longest river, flows through Warsaw.

There are several mountain ranges in the south of the country. They are the Sudety Mountains, the Tatra Mountains and the Carpathian Mountains. Many people like to walk in the mountains. Rysy Peak is the highest point in Poland.

This peak in the Tatra Mountains is known as the 'Sleeping Knight'. A folk tale says the knight will wake up when called to fight for his country.

Weather and seasons

Poland has four seasons: winter, spring, summer and autumn. Winters are cloudy and cold, with snow or rain. The coldest months are January and February. Spring is mild – not too hot and not too cold. Summers are warm and thunderstorms are common. July is usually the warmest and sunniest month. Autumn weather is crisp and sunny.

Rain is more common in summer than in other seasons.

Poles relax on a river beach. Many people head for the countryside in the summer.

🌀 **The snowy mountains of the south are great for winter sports, such as skiing.**

The weather is different from region to region. It is mildest on the coast, which also gets the most sunshine in summer. The weather is cooler and wetter in the mountains. Some peaks are covered with snow most of the year. In the north, where the lakes are, it is often cloudy.

Did you know?

Zakopane is known as the winter capital of Poland. Poles head south to this mountain town to ski.

Polish people

Poland is home to more than 38 million people. Almost all Polish people are descended from a group of people called Slavs. About 1,500 years ago, Slavs settled in the area that is now Poland. The Polish language comes from the old language of the Slavs. The Slavs were united under one king about 1,000 years ago.

Polish people celebrate their past in dance and music. They dance the mazurka and the polka. At festivals, they dress in colourful folk costumes.

Girls in folk costumes dance at a festival in Krakow.

People in Poland love fresh flowers. Flowers are sold on almost every street corner.

Did you know?

Wycinanki is the Polish word for paper cutting. People have decorated their homes with colourful paper cut-outs for more than 200 years.

Many Polish people like flowers. They grow flowers, sell them on the streets and give them as gifts. In spring, some people make paper cut-outs in the shape of flowers.

Religion is very important to the people of Poland. Most Poles are Roman Catholics. A few are Protestant, Muslim or Jewish.

Most people in Poland are Roman Catholic. This Catholic church is in the resort town of Zakopane.

School and family

After the Second World War, the government improved schools and made them free to all. Today, all children from the age of six to eighteen must attend. The school year runs from September to June. Primary school comes first. Then children go to secondary school.

Children study maths, history and science. They learn languages, including English. Some teenagers go to college to learn job skills. Others go on to study at university.

In primary school, children usually have one teacher for all their subjects.

On Sundays, many Polish families enjoy picnics in the park.

A Polish family enjoys a shared meal at the dinner table.

Family life is important in Poland. Children, parents and grandparents often live together. In many families, both parents work outside the home. On Sundays, people go to church and then relax. They might go for a picnic or a walk in a park or the countryside.

Did you know?

People in Poland celebrate Grandmother's Day and Grandfather's Day in January. Many children make or buy cards and small gifts for their grandparents.

Country

More than half of the land in Poland is used for farming. Most farms are small, narrow strips of land. Families live on the farms or in small villages nearby.

Many of the small farms still use horses to pull farm machinery and to pull carts. Some farmers use sharp, curved blades to harvest hay.

A small village sits among narrow strips of farm fields.

Workers use a tractor and trailer to harvest cabbages.

Poland is known for its fine horses. Arabian horses like these have been bred in Poland for hundreds of years.

Did you know?

More horses are bred in Poland than in any other country in Europe. People from around the world come to Poland to buy horses.

Farmers grow grain, sugar beet, potatoes and cabbages. They raise pigs, beef cattle and dairy cows, too. Farmers work long hours for small rewards and life is hard. Some farmers can only grow enough food for their families. Many young people move to cities to find other jobs.

City

Six out of every ten people in Poland live in big cities. Warsaw, the capital, has a population of almost two million people. It is the centre of business and government. Warsaw has new office buildings and tall skyscrapers alongside old town squares and pretty parks. People crowd the streets and outdoor markets. They ride buses, trams, bikes or motorbikes to work. Some drive small cars.

Did you know?

Trains connect most of the cities in Poland. It has one of the best train systems in Europe.

People in cities often use trams to travel to work. This tram runs along a main street in Warsaw.

People like to feed the pigeons in this square in Krakow. With its many markets and cafés, the main square is a centre of activity.

Fresh fruit and vegetables are sold in street markets, such as this one in Krakow.

Krakow, in the south, is another big city. It was once the capital of Poland. Tourists travel from all over the world to visit this beautiful city, packed with ancient buildings.

Gdańsk is a city on the Baltic coast. Ships bring goods in and out of the country at this seaport. Factories in Gdańsk make chemicals, machines, food products and cloth.

Polish homes

Poland is a crowded country and more homes are needed for people to live in. Many people live in tall blocks of flats in cities. Most of these flats are small, with only a few rooms. Many flats are built with a balcony.

Did you know?

In the past, some rich people lived in castles in Poland. The castles had as many as 100 rooms! Today, tourists enjoy visiting the castles.

In big cities, some people live in modern flats. These modern blocks are in Warsaw.

In the countryside, some people live in old houses. These are often built of wood as Poland has many forests. Most houses in the country are one-storey cottages, with two to four rooms. The kitchen might have a wood-burning stove for cooking and to heat water.

Some Polish houses are built for two or three families to share. They are made of brick or concrete. One family lives on each floor. Each family has a kitchen, a bathroom and bedrooms.

Food

Farming families grow most of the food they eat. Many people in Poland eat a lot of meat and vegetables. Cabbages and potatoes are often used in meals. Beef, sausages, pork, ham and chicken are popular, too.

Soup is the first course in most main meals. *Bigos* is a stew made of sausages, cabbage and mushrooms. *Pierogi*, or dumplings, are a popular meal, too. They are usually stuffed with meat, cabbage and mushrooms. Sometimes the filling is cheese, potato or fruit.

People buy Polish sausages from stalls in a Krakow market.

Borscht soup is a favourite dish in Poland, served hot or cold. It is made with beetroots, other vegetables and sometimes meat.

When the weather is good, diners crowd outdoor cafés in the cities.

In the cities, people shop at outdoor markets for fresh fruit and vegetables to cook at home. They eat out at cafés and restaurants. Many people enjoy fast foods, such as pizza and hamburgers.

Did you know?

Ice cream is a favourite dessert in Poland. It is called *lody*. Lody shops are common in the cities.

Having fun

People enjoy camping and fishing in Poland. They also like to walk and ski in the mountains. They like riding bicycles and horses, too. Sailing on the Baltic Sea is a popular pastime.

In the winter, children can enjoy tobogganing and skiing.

Polish people crowd the football stadiums to watch matches. Children of all ages enjoy playing football too. People watch basketball and boxing on television. Polish athletes compete in the Olympic Games.

Polish fans crowd a stadium to see their national football team play a match against Hungary.

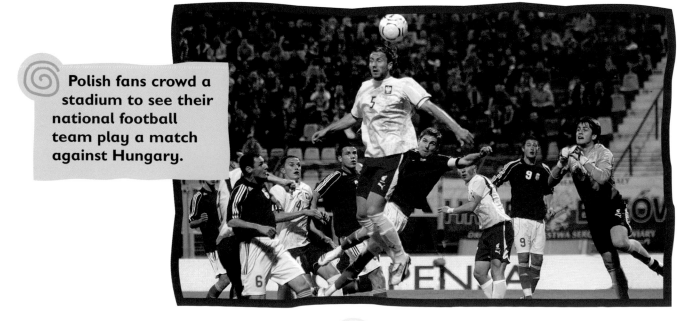

Did you know?

Poland has more than 20 national parks. They are great places for biking and walking.

For hundreds of years, village women have crafted lacework. They create delicate patterns for tablecloths and clothing. They stitch pretty designs on pillows and folk costumes. Men carve wooden boxes and spoons.

In the cities, many Poles go to festivals and watch films and plays. They like all types of music — classical, jazz and rock. Outdoor concerts are common in Warsaw, Krakow and other cities. People enjoy operas and ballets, too. They also like to visit museums.

Dancers perform a ballet at an old castle near Warsaw. Many people in Poland enjoy music and dance.

Poland: the facts

• Poland became a republic in 1918. Its official name is the Republic of Poland. After the Second World War, communists governed Poland. In 1990 Poland became a democracy.

• The president is the head of state. The prime minister is the head of the government. Laws are made by the National Assembly. The National Assembly is made up of the Senate and the Sejm.

• Polish citizens who are 18 years of age or older may vote. Presidential elections are held every five years.

• Poland is a very old country that was once ruled by kings.

• Poland joined the European Union in 2004.

The flag of Poland has two bars of red and white. White stands for honesty and kindness. Red stands for bravery.

• Many famous people came from Poland. The scientist Marie Curie was born in Warsaw. Frédéric Chopin was a great composer of classical music. Nicolaus Copernicus, a Polish scientist, is known as 'the father of astronomy'.

Did you know?

The white eagle is the symbol of Poland. When kings ruled Poland long ago, the eagle was shown on the flag.

The unit of money in Poland is the **zloty**. The country is expected to switch to the **euro** by 2014.

A flag with a white eagle hangs from a city hall building. The bird is a national symbol of Poland.

Glossary

Balcony an outside porch on an upper floor of a building.

Bog an area of wet land with rotting plants.

Chapel a room used for prayer or worship.

Coast an area of land that borders the sea.

Communist a person who believes that property should be owned by the community and each member of the country should work for the benefit of everyone.

Concrete a hard, strong building material.

Democracy where the government is elected by the people.

Dumplings dough that is boiled or steamed and sometimes filled with meat, vegetables or fruit.

Euro the unit of money of most countries in the European Union.

Head of state the main representative of a country.

Industry a business in which goods or products are made.

Mazurka a Polish folk dance.

Opera a play set to music.

Plains long stretches of flat land.

Prime minister the person who handles the day-to-day business of running the government.

Republic government in which decisions are made by the people of the country and their representatives.

Seaport a place on the coast where ships load and unload goods and passengers.

Tourists people who visit places for fun.

Trams vehicles that transport people on city streets. Trams run on rails or on strong overhead wires.

Zloty the unit of money in Poland.

Find out more

http://kids.nationalgeographic.com/Places/Find/Poland
This website gives a brief guide to Poland, with photographs.

www.bbc.co.uk/languages/other/quickfix/polish.shtmlw
A short introduction to Polish, with audio.

http://info-poland.buffalo.edu/classroom/ wycinanki/text.html
This website helps you to make your own Polish paper cut.

Note to parents and teachers: Every effort has been made by the Publishers to ensure that these websites are suitable for children, that they are of the highest educational value, and that they contain no inappropriate or offensive material. However, because of the nature of the Internet, it is impossible to guarantee that the contents of these sites will not be altered. We strongly advise that Internet access is supervised by a responsible adult.

Some Polish words

Polish is the official language of Poland. It is similar to Czech and Slovak.

Polish word	English word
Tak	Yes
Nie	No
Witamy!	Welcome!
Cześć	Hello
Do widzenia!	Goodbye
Nazywam się ...	My name is ...
Ile to kosztuje?	How much is it?
Nie rozumiem ...	I don't understand ...
Dobranoc	Goodnight
Proszę?	Please

My map of Poland

Trace this map, colour it in and use the map on page 5 to write the names of all the towns and cities.

Index